MW00436600

cope

Copyright © 2018 June Gehringer
All rights reserved.
Typesetting by Janice Lee
Cover Design by Michael Seidlinger
ISBN - 978-1-948700-12-2

THE ACCOMPLICES:
A Civil Coping Mechanisms Book
🐱 🐱 🐱

For more information, find CCM at:

http://copingmechanisms.net

I DON'T

WRITE

ABOUT RACE

BY JUNE GEHRINGER

for my mother and father.

"To understand just one life you have to swallow the world."
—Salman Rushdie

I. I don't write about race.

GAY 2
after Zoe Blair-Schlagenhauf

it's a sequel.
hooray.

we survived the first one,
some of us.

I don't write about race
for Daphne
after El Pearson

I don't write about race.

I don't talk about race.

My white friends are very supportive.

My white friends perform allyship on Facebook.

My white friends apologize, but neither
as often nor as profusely as
they should.

I hide my legs from the sun and
in the shower, they blend into
the off-white
mildew
off the walls.

I hide my legs from the
sun and in the
shower I try
to tell myself:
I'm not one of them.

The day after I graduated college, I took my white
father and my brown mother to the World
War II Museum and we sat
in silence as we read
that the Japanese killed 20
million Chinese people during World War
II.

(How many times have I been asked if I was Japanese?)

My brown mother and
I already knew this. I wonder
what my father knows.

I don't write about race,
I write about erasure.

I go to a bar with my white
sister and my brown brother. Someone
tells us that we all look
the same, and I wonder
what that means
for me, a white-brown
girl with an uncut
dick. But then I
remember
that I've heard this before, that
we all look the same.

I don't write about race,
I write about gender,
I once killed a cis white man,
and his first name
was me.

In Washington D.C., while walking
through the National Mall, I hear a white
teenager joyfully screaming with her
white friends.

In Washington D.C. I am terrified
to speak, I am terrified to
whisper. I write
poems on my phone instead.

I don't write about race,
I write about silence.

My white friends talk
about race. They say
all the right
words. I say
nothing.

I read poems about white
people to rooms full of white
people and they laugh
like they're in on the joke, they
laugh like they didn't
make me need
to write these poems.

In a poem I ask
white people everywhere
to please go
home. My white
audience laughs and
I wonder how much
of me is laughing
with them. I wonder
if my father is laughing
too.

I don't write about race,
I write about erasure.
I write only, and always
about myself.

for my mother

I love fireworks,
i'd love to see
jesus in
the street
turning
cop cars
into
anything.

faith
can be
such
a disappointment, someday
my mom
will hold
a book

with my name on the cover,
though not the one she chose.

dog person
for my dog

I tell my dog "sit" and he sits.
I tell my dog "stay" and he stays.
I tell my dog "dismantle" and he just looks at me.

We have both been trained
to do so many of the
wrong things.

I tell my dog to "stay" I tell
my dog "stay" to my dog i
tell to "stay" dog I tell, "stay"
tell "dog" my to to stay oh dog
tell me to stay good girl oh
dog please
stay.

etc.

a man looks
at me

etc.

Shoot for the moon
after El Pearson

If you miss,
try and hit a cop.

everyone at the coffeeshop is more beautiful than I am.

everyone at the coffeeshop is more beautiful than I am.

I think about lily and I think about el.

I try to think about killing anything other than myself.

tomorrow is the fourth of july.

so many
of the wrong things
are going to burn.

they always do.

someone somewhere
had their first kiss today, probably
many people did, probably
some of them were gay.

fuck it I guess I won't kill myself.

I think about closing my laptop but I don't.

I think about closing my laptop but I don't.

...

I haven't known what day it was in several days which seems impossible.

...

I don't know how to relate to people who spend fewer than ~4 hours a day on the internet and I'm not sure how to feel about that.

...

sitting across the street from a flower shop and watching people stop and try to pick out flowers and imagining who they're buying flowers for and hoping that none of them are dying but knowing that some of them are.

...

Marisa says that they'd like to open up a flower shop and I agree that running a flower shop sounds exciting and comforting as a possible way of life. each day I find myself wondering why I have chosen to live the way I live. I consider this briefly, before continuing to make the same choices over and over again.

...

marisa is eating something from a food truck. there was a parade today. there are puerto rican flags everywhere. I keep wishing el was here. the sun is hiding behind the buildings now and everything is gold and brown and wildly beautiful.

...

I feel a strange sense of inspiration which I think is coming from the sheer volume of human lives I have witnessed today. there are so many yellow and black and brown

bodies still alive and occasionally enjoying a happy
moment on a good day in the vicinity of a flower shop
where nobody has killed us yet.

...

I walk by a stream of water flowing from a burst hydrant
and a mother carefully steps around the largish moving
puddle and her child jumps in the puddle several times and
exuberantly to the mother's smiling indifference.

...

there are people living, everywhere. there are people living
here. "life has never seemed so possible" I tweet. I think
about closing my laptop, but I don't.

in a coffeeshop in brooklyn trying to find an original or interesting way to write about being in a coffeeshop in brooklyn.

...

I keep feeling that i'm living vicariously through myself. I get the vague sense that i'm doing what i'm doing in order to be able to tell myself that I did it. I love bragging about my friends but I don't have any friends so instead I brag about myself to myself.

...

I want to thank you all, profusely, for writing "FUCK DONALD TRUMP" in sharpie on the walls of every bathroom stall across the country. in a very serious way, I think there's a kind of poetry in that, a real and meaningful dialogue going on.

...

savannah, georgia looks like what I imagined new orleans would look like before I lived in new orleans. I'm wondering if, years from now, when I try to remember new orleans, i'll see savannah in my head. I'm not sure where our ideas of places come from. nothing is unforgettable.

"Sooooo many chanterelles in the woods this year!"

Gene is describing a lobster condo.

what a lobster condo is, according to gene, is a sheet of corrugated metal roughly the size of a garage door laid on cinderblocks on the ocean floor as a sort of cageless lobster trap.

according to gene, collecting lobsters from the lobster condo is a two-person operation. two people dive ~15 feet to the lobster condo. one lifts the metal sheet while the other hustles to collect as many lobsters as they can before the lobsters flee.

gene is convinced that I am a man.

the lobster harvesting process which gene has described is highly illegal, but I say that i'm rooting for him and I am.

an old college professor tweets a picture of mushrooms he collected in a forest near Leelanau, MI, while I try to defend my identity from white academics online. the mushrooms were yellow. they're called chanterelles.

Earlier Gene relayed an anecdote about being harassed on the bus. He seemed nervous as he attempted to relay, without seeming or sounding racist, that the man who harassed him was black. He described how another black man on the bus came to his defense. Gene carefully described how he felt, having been, he felt, legitimately threatened, and having been defended by a black man, saying "I don't think it's an 'us vs. them' situation", which seemed to imply both that Gene believed in the existence of a real and meaningful "us"/"them", and that he seemed to think that I was included in the "us."

Golden chanterelles are considered a delicacy, on the same tier of rare and delicious fungl as truffles. it's a strange thing about delicacies, that so many of them can be obtained for free, if one only knows the how and where. mushrooms on the forest floor. lobsters off the reef.

Gene describes Florida lobsters as having a taste that's almost identical to Maine lobsters. He says, however, that the flesh of the Florida lobster is quite firm as compared to the flesh of Maine lobsters. Gene says that he prefers this. He can't stomach the Maine lobsters, they're too soft. "They just fall apart," he says.

Gene lifts himself from the brown leather armchair directly across from the brown leather armchair I am seated in. He slowly lowers himself down to the main floor of the coffeeshop. He says that he's due for a procedure. "Double hip replacement", he explains. I wish him luck and shake his hand and he says not to worry. He says that for the first time in seven years, he'll be able to golf again.

I'm surprised by the sadness I feel when I realize that it's difficult for me to imagine that I will ever see Gene again. I imagine him floating, buoyant, between the florida keys. I imagine him diving 15 feet. I imagine Gene golfing underwater, swinging in slow motion, as if in outer space. I've heard that swimming is easier for those with chronic joint pain than walking. there's no impact. gene swings and the waves roll on above.

"im so bored" I think, as I watch congress make decisions which will affect millions of lives on my phone.

I get on the interstate and fantasize about hitting the car in front of me,
just to have someone to apologize to.

if everyone was as good as the best person I know, we still wouldn't be able to stop global warming.

this world is beyond saving.

thank god.

for Omaha

I can't remember the last time someone called me a chink.

I can remember the last time someone called me a faggot.

If you don't think language is a weapon,
be grateful no-one's pointing it at you.

White hands hover over
keyboards and pens,
White hands hover over
my neck,

don't tell me not to be afraid.
I know what white hands do.

I read one ignorant tweet and I think about it all day.

I don't care about gender,
I just wanna dress how I want,
fuck who I want,
and take drugs.

whenever someone was being a dick in the seventh grade,
they'd say:
"it's a free country",
and I think the principle holds true.

it's still a free country
if you're an immature little shit.

Everything I can

I promised myself
That I'd do everything I could.

I don't want to have kids but I know
there will be kids.

The world should be
Better, mom, I'm doing
Everything I can I can't
Get out of bed

Lying on my back I raise
A fist toward the shaking
Ceiling fan.

I'm doing everything I can.

there's a parade outside and I can hear people singing from the bathroom.

on the last refrain, one of the altos dropped the sickest harmony line.

all this and im sitting on the toilet
thinking of everyone I miss and how
there are people who love me 1000 miles
in any direction.

I love this life,
I swear I do.

II. my father sells insurance/a well trained dog.

goes to the supermarket still coming down and asks which things are vegan and which things aren't vegan and nobody who works there is really sure how to answer, and shouldn't she, as a vegan, be able to tell which things are and aren't vegan to which she responds that she actually isn't vegan, she's just wondering which things are and aren't vegan.

goes home with a tub of vegan cookie dough and a case of La Croix and almost hits a squirrel in her neighborhood and screeches to a halt and gets honked at by the car behind her and touches her fingers to the bridge of her nose, drives around the block another time before pulling into the parking lot.

carries the things upstairs and rearranges the cushions on the couch. rearranges the plants on top of the bookshelf. thinks about rearranging the furniture but doesn't rearrange the furniture. yellow rug. lots of shit on the coffee table.

rolls a joint and listens to a podcast about scientology and thinks, "those people, what happened to them." takes a hit of the joint and thinks "what happened to me." thinks about taking a shower but can't take a shower until finished with the joint. finishes the joint and takes a shower.

realizes she's a bit too high. sits down in the shower and grabs at her knees. the water gets cold.

sits on the couch and realizes that she didn't get the the stuff she needed from the supermarket but can't remember what things they were. a toothbrush? tries to remember something else but can't. tries but can't.

flips past televangelists on tv. joel osteen. somebody who looks a lot like joel osteen. thinks about the way she looks and isn't sure whether or not she looks like herself. isn't sure if that makes sense.

wants to eat something but all she has is vegan cookie dough and nobody to call. three weeks left in this apartment.

goes to work the next day and phones it in. I mean really phones it in. doesn't bother to shower. her boss says something, in response to which she just says "so". gets sent home. is told to come back with a better attitude. assumes this means she won't be coming back at all.

on the way home listens to "Tallahassee" by the Mountain Goats and thinks "this album kinds of sucks" and turns it up. smokes a joint with the windows rolled up. the last time she rolled her window down it fell into the door. she doesn't trust it anymore.

needs someone to call but doesn't have anyone to call. in between hits she mumbles "I think i'm going to lose my job." the air conditioner hums as it blows the smoke around the car while the guy from the mountain goats sings about a house falling into disrepair and a room full of fabulous prizes. on the way home she drives past a hobby lobby and wishes she had a hobby but can't imagine a hobby she'd enjoy.

gets home again and realizes she needs to talk to verizon customer service. she's been putting this off. thinks the phone is broken but isn't sure. it makes calls and sends texts, but it doesn't receive anything. she has to go on facebook to talk to anyone. which isn't working out. has to call verizon, but can't or won't.

assume i'm everywhere
and love me like I am.

love me
like I leave the house.

you have to unlearn so much in order to be happy.
I keep forgetting
the wrong things
where I left my keys, and
how to call my mom - how many times
Did I say I would? I don't know how
to unlock
my phone.

you have to unlearn so much in order to be happy,
but I am so busy
with forgetting
that I forgot
to fuck or eat or not
forget the names of stars.

I want to sit on the beach and love something.
I can't understand what's happening to me
well enough to do anything about it.

instead of writing i've taken to getting
too drunk to remember
the way the men
have looked at me.

Prometheus as queer icon:

The worst part is
he healed.
Each night the fucker healed, just
to be maimed anew.

Would have saved himself a lot of time,
if he'd had the good sense just to die.

you have to wonder
how many caterpillars die
mid-metaphor.

it's so easy to forget the time that healing takes,
so hard to remember worms
when one
sees a butterfly.

the physicists have informed me that the universe is curved.
parallel lines do not exist.

it's 2017.
none of y'all are straight.

my father sells insurance.

when I heard that john mccain had cancer I thought of my
  father.
my dad paid for the house I grew up in by selling health
  insurance
to the kind of people who buy health insurance from people
who remind you of john mccain, which is not to say that my
father is an evil man, but rather to say that he's the kind
of man you say yes to.

my dad never fought in any war but that didn't stop him
from getting cancer, didn't stop him from drinking like a
  white man with
regret, which is not to say that he didn't have regret, but he did
have cancer. he did. and he drank like it.

which isn't to say that he doesn't still drink like a murderer,
  doesn't
drink like cancer, this is not to say that he or I or john mccain is
innocent. we're too american for that, which is really just
another way of saying that we're complicit, that john mccain
is the kind of man you say yes to, that I am a tumor
found too late, and my father
is a quiet old man
who once
very long ago
refused to leave his cell.

I don't know what kind of person marco polo was
but I want somebody to blame.

Anxiety is a house where I live with my hot amazing friends.

Hello,
Welcome to my house.

I live here with my hot amazing friends.

We don't go outside.

I keep wanting to go somewhere.
how funny is that?

I haven't had a thought in weeks.

my roommate three roommates ago was worried I'd get bedsores from spending so much time in bed.
she'd say, "i'm worried you're going to get bedsores from spending so much time in bed."
& I would laugh.
& I am laughing now.

2017 was the year I wanted to know anything about myself
that didn't include the fact that thousands, maybe millions of
people online and irl would like to see me dead.

I can't tell you what I learned in 2017 i
couldn't tell the difference between imperfection
and hell couldn't tell discomfort from harm, in 2017 I couldn't
  tell you
so I just
didn't so i
just
kept going
anywhere I could.

I drove the country twice just looking
for thirty minutes
in which I felt alright.

I want to tell you I found it.

I really do.

remembering random instances of racism from your childhood and struggling to remain calm while talking to your mom on the phone in the car on the way to work.

For A.

maybe the best thing about me
is for two nights in savannah, GA three months and five
thousand miles apart from each other,
I meant something to anyone.

i'm hoping it was you.

when I ask what you're doing with the rest of your life you laugh even though we both know i'm not joking and you're merciful enough not to ask the same thing back it feels nice to think of people without going online.

life as a kind of escape.
i'd go anywhere with you.

the first time it happened was in school. I think Nick even had the same bookbag as me. the same. and how to remember which was mine? how not to grab the wrong bag and bring it to the wrong home, the wrong family?

it almost happened to me once. I was maybe seven. I got sick in school. I was always sick in school. the teachers made me bring my own boxes of tissues. always thinking too much. always puking, always blowing my nose.

but so I got sick in school. and becky kafka walked me to the office, to, I don't know, make sure I didn't pass out on the stairs and crack my head on the lino floor. and I went to the office and sat in the office. and the secretary called the wrong set of parents. the wrong mom showed up to pick me up. and she was mad.

I went to a small catholic school in nebraska and the office secretary called the wrong set of parents. which maybe would have fallen into the "permissible but mind-boggling" category of administrative fuckup, had the secretary not mistakenly called the parents of the only other asian kid at St. Bernards. I don't remember if the secretary (Mrs. Peters?) got fired for that, but i'm inclined to think that she should have been. or maybe not. she was a sweet woman, no malice in her intent. and yet.

I remember sitting in the plastic kid-sized chair while Nick's mother gave Mrs. Peters an almost proverbial chewing-out, and thinking that it was all my fault. Mrs. Peters had been kind to me, would wait with me in the afternoons when my parents were late coming to pick me up, which was often (which, then, shouldn't she have known which one I was?). We were all always late. And she was kind. What fault of hers was it that this white woman didn't know my name?

I felt all the guilt that my tiny, vomitously empty body could feel. The guilt, perhaps, of a well-trained dog.

III. Leviathan.

this is a story all about how
my life got flip-turned upside-down
and i'd like to take a minute, just sit right there
and i'll tell you how I became the prince
of a town called
clinical depression

Hey r u a cool ranch Dorito?

Bc u r beloved by many and generally regarded to b a very good thing!

When my boss interviewed me for my job he asked
are you a lifer?

And I said
yeah.

This is what I want to do.

When I came out to my mom I said
Mom,
I'm trans.

she said
Okay.
What does that mean?

I wanted so badly to say
Mom,
I thought you could tell me.

I didn't say anything.

My mom said *are you there?*

And I said *yes,*
this is me.

what else
Do you say?

Leviathan.

You go to the bar hoping something good might happen.
You don't know what.

nothing does. You buy another drink in hopes. And nothing
   does. And nothing good
continues to happen. to you, somewhat pointedly, you feel.

And something does and smiles at you. They smile at you.
   you think:
This is the good thing.

you go home. You go to someone's home. You're at home.
You are at someone's home and smiling. At them. At you. At
all of it.

And someone kisses you at which point you know the rest.
Or think you do. you assume.

This is gratuitous, you think. *If I know you like me and you
know I like you then do we really have to do this? What
point is left to prove?* You find a tongue between your
teeth. You find two tongues between your teeth. You find a
tongue. You find someone.

The rest is denouement. All the fun is in finding. In
discovery. In imagining a body which might fit into yours.
And doesn't quite. But does and so you do. And it does. It
does. It does. For how long? For long enough. And was it
something good. Wasn't it? Something? Something good?

At my parents' house,
watching *Viceland* with my mom.

It's 2018.
Is loving your friends still cool?
Idk what else to do.

(poem for post-traumatic growth)

WHEN YOU TEAR A PIECE OF PAPER IN HALF YOU ACTUALLY HAVE MORE PIECES OF PAPER

excuse me if I'm a little rough around my edges

The reason I crave intimacy is not because I actually want to know or be known but rather because I'm a master self-destructor and the easiest way to really fuck myself up is getting close to someone else

Every time I see a cis girl I want to kill myself.
Too depressed to see my friends.
If you could cut my shoulders in half would you?

"You look lovely."

"Thanks."

It's your side of the bed until it isn't anymore.

The lousy window is still there and light is coming through and there's birds and trees and shit.

The birds are singing a really shitty song.

The trees were there before it was your side of the bed.

I imagine the trees are laughing at me but I realize that they're too old to care. The trees have shit to do.

The birds have shit to do. The lady walking her pug in a stroller has shit to do. Everyone has shit to do but me.

I roll over onto the not-your-side of the bed. lying on my back I stick my tongue out at the ugly lousy trees.

I can't believe how suck they are.

I look over at the trees to see if they've noticed and they haven't and I close my eyes and eventually the day passes.

Hey u wanna hear a joke?
For foster

Cmon.
It's a really good joke.
You'll like it.
It's not like my other jokes.

I know your cat is sick.
Cmon.
It's a really good joke.

It goes like this:
there are many people who love and value you and who
believe in you and there's a ton of beautiful shit in the world
worth living for and the punchline is it's actually not a joke
these are just true facts about life in the universe.

Your cat is going to live forever.
Everybody's cat will live forever.
And everyone we love will get jobs and will not die,
And 2017 will end,
And everything will end.
And those people,
I'm one of them,
I am every one.

I don't miss dating you, I miss
having someone to be nice to.

I mean, I do miss dating you, in that
I miss having something to like about myself.

I could fall in love with anyone.
I really could.

A dead girl

Is a girl is a girl is a girl.

The Washington post says something about how *his* parents
loved *him*.

The us government knows something about nothing,
Knows a whole hell of a lot about nothing,
Knows what they could guess about between
her legs,

which guesses dictate,
As guesses often do,
The way the Washington post talks
About a girl,
About the girls,
About the women
who will never serve,
thank god,
The government has tried to kill us every other way,
But we will never serve
 the government or god or
death, which is all the same
I think.

We're alive right now,
Some of us,
Which is all I could ask:
I mean sure,
I could ask for much more,
But it's all I'll get.

when the census taker comes
I'll tell them:
I am alive
In America
Somehow.

And they'll say *sir*
And I'll say *yes,*
and we will both survive.

I wear my crocs to the bar
The bartender is playing arcade fire
Everything is a tiny circle
Whoever you were in 2009
Etc etc etc

Leviathan.

You go to the bar.
again.

You know that nothing good will happen.

someone looks at you and you try to convince yourself of
  something.

You go to the bar and buy a tequila shot for someone else.
  It doesn't help.

you do it again. And go home to filthy sheets and empty
  cups and dell containers strewn around your bed.

You go home to filthy sheets and think, "is this it? Is this all
  there is?"

You fall asleep. You wake up. You do it again. Until you
  can't. or won't.

Oh god no.

Not the military.

What's next?

Is the government gonna ban me from Quiznos?

Leviathan.

The band is always too loud. You can't remember shit.

You write nothing for months and pretend to be a poet.

You attempt to remember something you don't have a name for. *Youth* or *love* or *life*. *Joy*, you decide. That's the thing I'm missing.

You consume drugs in pursuit of the nameless thing which you call *joy*.

You want to change your name but don't. It didn't fix anything the first time.

You think of moving to Philadelphia. All your friends live in Philadelphia. Everyone hates you here, you're absolutely sure.

You realize that there's nowhere on earth where you would be happy, no time or place in which you could ever not be you. You come to terms with this, and decide to revel in your own unhappiness.

You proceed to do so for several years.

Leviathan.

Over drinks with an old friend you remark that nothing feels the same. And she tells you something which you can't quite hear.

You say, "thanks. It helps."

Leviathan.

You get older.
You make regrettable decisions on purpose,
that in your old age you might have something to regret.

How many millions wish you dead?
You yourself one among them, another white
man's voice.

You get so busy with survival
that you forget to live.

You use whichever bathroom you feel
least likely
to get your ass kicked in.

You reconcile yourself to this.
You reconcile yourself to *it*.

it is nothing new. You go again
to the bar and
somehow
the day ends.

I let my tires go flat on purpose,
hoping to rear-end somebody:
wanting to apologize,
again and again and again.

I feel most like myself
when I feel guilty
for occupying
space.

It's not that I don't
write about race,
it's that I can't,
or won't.

I've spoken up enough:
these days I wish
that I
was not a girl.

How easy would it be?

There's so much I'll never know.

I won't let you eat my ass:
I can't stand to think of all it's not.

It's going to sound absurd,
but I went off social media

because the word "bussy"
was making me depressed.

Hymn I.

"This is not
a life. This is
not my life, this
is not

a life."

After John cougar mellencamp.

Oh yeaaaaaaa life goes on,
long after the thrill
of living
is gone.

Hahaha lmao wyd after this???

IS GONE IS GONE IS GONE

After Daphne Calhoun and Faye Chevalier.

Isn't here, must be somewhere?
Must be nice. Must be fucking
nice.

You spend years looking for the thing and
dig up
pictures
of your mom
when she was young
and happy.

presumably.

it isn't here and isn't there,
is gone is gone is gone,
the singer sings too loud,
a dog or song you haven't heard,
and don't care to,
don't care to, don't
care, too, don't care,
to, you just

don't care or
can't,
or won't.

Leviathan.

You drive by your ex's house each day
on your way to work.

You want to feel something,
but don't.

"Surely this," you thought. You keep on hoping
that she'll be there,
walking to her car
smoking a cigarette,
just to fuck you up,
but nothing does.

You try to hurt yourself but lose resolve.
You try to hurt yourself with friends and drugs and drinks
and
sharper things,
but nothing does.

You buy a honing steel and a whetstone.
You sharpen your knives before you cook,
Which at least you cook.

You try to push a dull knife through an onion and feel
grateful when it slips.
You burn yourself cleaning the grill at work and feel
grateful for the opportunity
to scream, feel grateful to be asked
What happened? Are you ok?
to have something to point to,
some red and blistered skin,
to feel justified, as
through tears,
you say:

No,
I'm not.
I'm fucking not.

Leviathan.

You try to summon something and for once,
you know exactly what.

Leviathan. An eidolon from a long-lost age.

You fancy yourself a character in a JRPG.
You fancy yourself a Japanese character in a Japanese
  video game,
which is exactly
as fucked up as it seems.

You are aware of this.

You are everything
you hate, which is to say
you are yourself.

You are not a Japanese character
in a Japanese video game.

You are not Chinese.
You are not even white.

You fancy yourself a character
in the movie of your life,
which nobody would watch,
because it is your life.

(Starring Scarlett Johansson because *of fucking course.*)

Your great grandparents fled genocide,
so that in a foreign country you might try
and fail
to escape
yourself.

You fancy yourself a summoner,
one who brings back things long dead,
one who has been traumatized,
and who is still alive.

Leviathan, in all your wrath:
Wreak hell of hell
I've wrought.

(Lacking cosmogony you attempt
to make
your own. You summon
Your own gods.
You cook
each day.
It helps. However
 much.)

Hell, you're told,
is a place inside your head.

so is everywhere,
you think.

Hymn II.

All of this should burn.
All of us should drown.

Leviathan.

After j Jennifer Espinoza and never angel north.

bring to us
the end that we deserve.

Drown me in my sin:
I am a girl
who has lived too long.

Some of us are here,
and some of us are not.
I will be here tomorrow,
but some of us will not.

The band is still too loud, thank god,
to loud to hear the end: the water
comes. And comes, she
comes.

Leviathan, a girl who has been,
alive too long:

And has seen the things the men will do,
and has had enough.

She will drown us all.
Thank god, thank god, thank god.

All Creation.
After JI Yoon Lee.

I.

How to
destroy the enemy
when the enemy is us?

If I can't unlearn,
I am to die.
Everything I hate is in my blood:

My father's blood, my mother's, too,
Whiteness has less to do with anything
than one's willingness
to forget.

(How many times have I referred
to Asian people as "Asian
People", as if "we" are one thing?)

II.

the enemy is in the mirror,
telling me I'm him.

Writing poems at the bar, writing
always at the bar, trying
still,
to care,

to find
a word in English,
to call myself,
not knowing any in Chinese.

Hymn III.

Hey you wanna FUCK?!?

F eel empathy and
U nderstanding for
C one another and take joy in learning
K and growing together, in spite of everything.

Leviathan.

is forgetting to call your mom;
is not a well trained dog;
is remembering random instances of racism from childhood,
  and struggling to remain calm;
is a dead girl;
is a girl is a girl;
is a girl who has been alive too long;
is everything between her legs;
and everything that's not;

means nothing in Chinese;
means nothing to anyone but me;
means nothing to anyone including me;
is the enemy is you is me;
wishes she was not a girl;
has felt the ways the men have looked at her;
carries a knife and a taser;
is never surprised;

is alive.
is still alive.
somehow.

Leviathan.

Your mother
comes to see you
at work
and uses
a name
you haven't heard
in years.

You smile as you flip
an egg.

The world
turns
with you
attached.

Author's Note:

This book was written in an attempt to understand myself, a mixed Chinese and white trans woman surviving nomadically in the United States of America.

Having finished the book, I don't feel I understand myself any more than I did when I began. Rather, I have realized that my identity is too complex to be understood. The best I can hope for, I think, is to be able to give voice to my complication and my confusion. To accept, and to be able to take comfort in the ambiguity that forms the core of who I am.

If this book was frustrating or disappointing to read, it is because it was in many ways frustrating and disappointing to write, perhaps necessarily so. I am learning, or trying to. Thanks for bearing with.

Wishes,
June

About the author.

Born and raised in Omaha, NE, JUNE GEHRINGER is a mixed Chinese trans woman who is somehow still alive. She is the author of *I love you it looks like rain* (Be About It 2017), and *EVERYONE IS A BIG BUG TO SOMEONE* (self-published) 2017. She is the co-founder of *tenderness yea*, and tweets @unlovablehottie. She holds a B.A. in English from Loyola University New Orleans and has worked as a cook since she was 16.

Acknowledgments.

some of these poems originally appeared in *Paper Darts*, *The Wanderer*, *Peach Mag*, and *Bad Nudes*. thank u.

thank u Zoë and Amelia.

thank u Laura and Taylor.

thank u CCM.

thank u Be About It.

thank u mom.

thank u dad.

Go love something while u can u fucken nerd.

OFFICIAL

CCM ◕

GET OUT OF JAIL
* VOUCHER *

- -

Tear this out.

Skip that social event.

It's okay.

You don't have to go if you don't want to. Pick up
the book you just bought. Open to the first page.
You'll thank us by the third paragraph.

If friends ask why you were a no-show, show them
this voucher.
You'll be fine.

- -

We're coping.

◕

CPSIA information can be obtained
at www.ICGtesting.com
Printed in the USA
LVHW11s1423021018
591987LV00033B/567/P